I'M NOT THE
BOSS

I just work here

---

*Insights and lessons from the founder
of America's #1 telecom company*

I'M NOT THE
BOSS

I just work here

Insights and lessons from the founder
of America's #1 telecom company

HOWARD JONAS
*founder and chairman
of IDT Corp.*

LEVIATHAN PRESS
BOOKS THAT MAKE A DIFFERENCE

I'm Not THE BOSS
I Just Work Here

© Copyright 2004 Howard Jonas

Leviathan Press
17 Warren Road, Suite 16A
Baltimore, Maryland 21208
410-653-0300

Library of Congress Cataloging-in-Publication Data

Jonas, Howard.
  I'm Not The Boss, I just work here : insights and lessons
from the founder of America's #1 telecom company / by
Howard Jonas.
     p. cm.
  ISBN 1-932443-05-3
  1. Jonas, Howard—Anecdotes. 2. Judaism—Doctrines.
3. Ethics, Jewish. I. Title.
  E184.37.J66A3 2004
  296'.092—dc22

                                    2003017765

Distributed by
The Judaica Press, Inc.
718-972-6200   800-972-6201
info@judaicapress.com
www.judaicapress.com

Manufactured in the United States of America

Table of Contents

foreword

I WAS FOURTEEN WHEN I STARTED SELLING HOT dogs on a street corner in the Bronx. I built my own stand with my father in the garage, and the business was a hit. Now, at forty-seven, I run a multi-billion dollar telecommunications company that ranks among the largest in the world—but now I have to pay if I want a hot dog.

People tend to be impressed by "success stories" like mine. Although the story is mine, the success is not. As the book cover says—I just work here. I may be riding on top of the world right now, but I'm intensely aware that it could all come to an end tomorrow. In my own life, I've gone through so many ups and downs that I'd be a fool to think otherwise. Life has taught me to recognize that I'm not really in charge, that I'm not the One pulling the strings.

The truth is, I look at life differently than most people I know. I've certainly been called a lot of things in my life: quirky, unorthodox, a maverick—just to name a few—and the ideas in this book might seem a little peculiar to you at first. So try to hang on for the ride, and if you think you haven't learned anything by the time you're done, just let me know. Maybe I'll buy you a hot dog.

[*o n e*]

The great blackout of 1965

IN 1313 B.C.E., AMIDST THUNDER AND LIGHTNING, G-d revealed Himself to the Israelites. They actually heard Him speak as He began to hand down the Ten Commandments. The rest of the world largely ignored these commandments, and the part about actually hearing G-d speak was attributed by the nations to an over-reaction to some adverse weather conditions.

Nothing of similar significance happened for the next few millennia until—amidst thunder and lightning—the Big Bertha power plant in New York went out, setting off a chain reaction of power failures that plunged the entire northeast of the United States into the great blackout of 1965. Similar to the blackout of 2003, for a whole night civilized men and women were reduced to desert nomads as television, radios, electric lights—all the products of thousands of years of progress—ceased to function. Once power was restored, however, mankind went right back to its old ways and, once again, attributed the experience to adverse weather conditions.

I, however, know for certain that neither event had anything whatsoever to do with meteorology. The record needs to be set straight. Mankind deserves to know the truth. It's time for me, once and for all, to reveal what I know.

In the fall of 1965, I was attending P.S. 32 in the Bronx. Each morning I'd board a dull yellow school bus that would whisk me off to school. As far as I was concerned, there was only one good thing about school—going home. Better yet, not going home. My mother, you see, wasn't home on the afternoon of November 9 to pick me up at the bus stop. She was working. So, instead, I was dropped off at my dad's storefront insurance office. Now this was fun.

Here, I could play stoopball with the Puerto Rican kids, attend story hour at the local public library and buy cuchifritos, Cokes and Wise onion garlic potato chips at the corner bodega.

Rosado, the bodega owner, would even pay me two cents for every small deposit Coke bottle I brought him, and five cents for the large ones. The secretaries' trash cans in my father's office were always full of these bottles. I was in cuchifrito heaven.

Not that life at my father's office was all play. Not at all. As far as I was concerned, an office was a place for work. But I already knew that work was much more fun than play. That was why adults went to work and kids got sent to school. At work you could do lots of fun things like seal envelopes, run mail through the postage meter, put folders in alphabetical order and operate the cash register. What a blast! There was nothing as fun as doing these things with the secretaries.

Most of the secretaries, like Ann, Rose and Eileen, were happy to have my help (or, with thirty-eight years hindsight, they were nice enough to take the trouble to indulge a cute nine-year-old boy who wanted to help).

Matilda was another story. Boy, was she mean. She sat at the front desk because she was the office manager. All the other secretaries had to pay homage to her and cater to her every whim. All Matilda wanted them to do was work. The less talking, the less time spent on coffee breaks, the more clickity-clack of the typewriter, the happier the dowager princess was. Everything in her kingdom had been going perfectly well until a certain nine-year-old boy came along. She would have had the police take me away as a trespasser or a vagrant, but for the fact that I was the boss's son; a troublesome irritant that had to be tolerated. I was tolerated but severely confined.

"Little boys can't touch electric typewriters," she would tell me. "They might lose their fingers playing with the keys."

So it was the manual typewriter only.

"Little boys can't put envelopes in the postage meter," she would say. "They might get ink on their hands and die of lead poisoning."

Death was an ever-present reality in this office. (Why else did people need insurance?) I imagined that little boys I knew were probably dying at offices all over the Bronx.

In the back room there were two sets of files, the live files in the new cabinets where the doors rolled out easily, and the dead files in the old overstuffed cabinets where the metal groaned when the file drawers were dragged open. Those dead files really scared me. True, being assigned to the dead files usually only meant someone had moved his business to another insurance broker. But to me, as a young boy, having your file moved to that cabinet meant you had probably died a horrible death and they had just finished shoveling the dirt onto your coffin. Almost forty years later, I still have that same feeling about clients who move their business elsewhere.

Back to Matilda. I had to be very careful around this lady. With time, though, I found that if I appeared serious, polite and diligent in performing my tasks, I could still have fun working and even slip notes to the secretaries about all the nasty things I'd like to do to Matilda. Just as long as I didn't go near anything dangerous.

Imagine Matilda's reaction when, after disembarking from the bus this fine November day,

I sat down on the client side of the counter in the office, next to the high-speed electric fan (which was off), and began to spin the blade with my fingers.

"Stop that," she shrieked, "you'll cut your fingers off."

"No I won't, the fan's not on," I retorted.

"Stop that at once, you miscreant. I said stop that now."

"You can't tell me what to do, Captain Hook. I'm not in your office. I'm a customer. You're not the boss here."

"You stop that at once or I'll get your father."

"Ha, ha, ha, I just saw him drive away." (Either the devil had gotten into me that day or, like many an oppressed freedom fighter, the little dictator had finally pushed me too far, and I had decided to assert my rights once and for all.)

"The fan could just come on suddenly and you'll lose your fingers and never be able to play ball," she cajoled, sensing that perhaps reason, not force, would appeal to me now.

"No it won't. Off is off," I replied.

"Well, if you keep spinning the fan backward

without turning it on, you'll blow all the electricity and none of the electric typewriters will work."

What? Where'd she come up with that? I thought back on all the Mr. Wizard TV shows I'd ever seen. I remembered everything that my father, a former TV repairman, had taught me about electric circuitry. I'd never heard anything like this before. I mean, something this major about the consequences of spinning an electric fan backwards, I would surely have heard about it. Right? Nah. I decided she must be bluffing. "You're making it up. Liar, liar, pants on fire. See, I'm spinning and spinning and nothing is happening and…"

And then suddenly the lights went out. Uh-oh, I remember thinking. Now I'd done it.

"Now see what you did," she snarled triumphantly. "I'll have to change the fuse myself and boy are you gonna get it when your dad gets back! Now I have to go to Rosado and buy some new fuses."

Before she could get up to go, Rosado came running in, with my father just behind him.

"Have you lost power too?" he said. "Must be the whole building's out." Before Matilda could turn me in, Dad suggested that they go change the main fuse in Berel the shoemaker's store to get the power back. It was already past five, so Matilda and the other secretaries left, giving me time to explain my offense in a way most likely to get me in the least trouble. After all, I reasoned, what's the real damage?

The power didn't come back, though. Changing the fuse didn't work for my dad. Nor did it work for any of the other neighborhood storeowners who came running over to see if we'd lost power also. Luigi the pizza man, Fred the mattress man, Dominic from the fruit store. All without power. The whole of East 180th Street in the Bronx—powerless. Nothing was going to save me now! Why hadn't I just left the darned fan alone?

But it was only as my father and I drove home that I began to see the enormity of what I'd done. All the traffic lights in the Bronx were out. Police officers were directing traffic. There were no lights on anywhere and night was falling. Boy, I'd really done it this time!

When I arrived home, everyone seemed to be running around with transistor radios glued to their ears, or buying out the stores' supplies of candles, flashlights and batteries, as well as milk, bread and other staples, as the news spread that the entire Northeast had lost power.

Then the greatest block party in history began. People stayed up all night picnicking together by flashlight. Neighbors who hadn't seen each other for years came together with wine, cheese and cookies. The crime rate that magical evening fell to zero, as everyone pulled together. For one magical evening, mankind became a brotherhood and those forgotten Ten Commandments actually seemed to be in force. Our house actually became one of the partying centers. My father's camping lantern and propane stove, which previously had only attracted mosquitoes to our campsite whenever we went camping, now attracted happy neighbors to our apartment.

Once the lights came back on, everyone's attention focused on a single question: Why had the power gone out? Con Ed, the largest power company in the United States, came under the scrutiny of politicians, regulators, civic leaders and the press. Was the company somehow at fault? Had they asked for rate increase after rate increase, all the while mismanaging construction of the nation's power grid? Had adequate safeguards been overlooked in the interest of profit?

One wrong answer and Con Ed would be finished. Its executives would be summarily dismissed. No more rate increases. Maybe even a state takeover of the power industry. So what did Con Ed do at this crucial juncture?

What could it do? It blamed the weather. Sure, who could fault it for a freak lightning storm that knocked out its main generator? I mean, nobody could plan for that. It's like being struck by lightning, if you know what I mean. Like I said, whenever reality is just too much to accept, people blame the weather.

Me, I was thrilled. I had been sure that at any minute the FBI would find out about the fan and take me away, probably for good. I mean, an event this big... Every detective in the United States had probably been dispatched and had already traced the outage to East 180th Street in the Bronx, maybe even to my father's store. Man, the minute those investigators called Matilda, she'd start singing like a canary. Yeah, no pressure would be necessary to get her to rat on me. Why, she probably called the FBI herself to report me. Yup, no question about it, I was cooked.

And then, just as I was getting ready to spend the rest of my youth in some reform school with Jimmy Cagney and his gang, the lightning story comes out. First, just a tip passed on by a reporter at an all-news station; then, a confirmed scoop by the Associated Press. Finally, the official announcement from Con Ed. Soon it was everywhere—TV, radio, the newspapers. Now everyone believed that lightning caused the blackout. The police were probably going to send a paddy wagon to take Matilda with her fan story off to the nuthouse. Ah, sweet deliverance!

Of course, for a few days I was still a little

nervous. For sure, Con Ed had pinpointed my dad's office by now. But as one day passed and then another, it became obvious that even if Con Ed knew the truth, it was just going to stay our little secret. And that was just fine with me.

For years, I walked around convinced that it was I who had caused the great blackout of 1965. Even while everyone around me was still blaming the weather: The weather had caused the blackout, and the weather was responsible for what had happened at Mount Sinai over three thousand years ago.

It took a while, but eventually I realized that I was not to blame for the blackout. I also eventually realized that weather was not the culprit for the events at Mount Sinai. G-d actually spoke there. He really did give the Ten Commandments and the Bible there, and I can prove it. Read on, and I'll explain.

two

A *new world*

UNTIL SECOND GRADE I LIVED IN A NEAR PERFECT world. Everyone in our middle-class neighborhood was prospering and moving up. America was at peace. President Kennedy was always frolicking on one beach or another with his good-looking wife and young kids. Mickey Mantle and the Yankees had just won another World Series. Then, one November day, it all started to come apart.

Miss Salvatico, my second grade teacher, told the class that we must all be strong and pray for the country and remain quiet while Dr. Hayes, our principal, made a special announcement over the P.A. system to the school. Dr. Hayes got on and said, "Students of P.S. 32, I have a very sad announcement to make. We have just been informed by the Board of Education that President Kennedy has been shot in Dallas. Please remain in class with your teachers and let us all say the Pledge of Allegiance and hope for the best." Miss Salvatico led us in the Pledge, then asked us to open our workbooks and work silently on that night's homework assignment. I looked up and saw her begin to cry before running into the hallway to embrace an older, matronly teacher who was also collapsing in tears. My innocence (and the whole country's, as well) was over.

Returning from school, I saw people huddled together, some gathering around policemen and others sitting in their cars with their radios on. The word not spoken in school was whispered over and over again on the streets. Dead. The President is dead. Kennedy is dead. But I wouldn't listen. I wouldn't allow myself to hear. "If I don't listen," I told myself, "if I don't hear, he'll get better." I believed that the same way I believed that I'd be protected from appendicitis if I didn't know which side my appendix was on.

When I arrived home and found my mother collapsed, weeping on the floor in front of the black and white TV, I knew it was over. "They killed him," she wailed again and again. "They killed him. Why is it always the good ones who get it? They killed him. They killed our President."

I needed an answer. I wanted an answer. But I had no answer. There was no escape. Not even to cartoons. For days there was nothing but the funeral. The President's horse. John John saluting. The unbelievable televised assassination of the murderer Oswald. And then Arlington. Twenty-one guns.

Later, the cartoons returned and we all tried to get back to normal, to pretend it was just the weather. A freak lightning strike in an otherwise peaceful day.

But the storm did not abate. The next year, the Yankees lost to the Cards in the seventh game of the World Series. Five years later, Martin Luther King, Jr. was shot and the country erupted into race riots. Then Robert F. Kennedy was gunned down. Then the Yankees fell to ninth place. Then Vietnam. Mantle's ailing knees finally gave out for good and he retired from the game. Soon, not just the ghetto but the campus, the parks, the whole country seemed to be coming apart. Tear gas, unemployment, drugs everywhere. White flight, black rage. Body bags. Love it or leave it. Ho Ho Ho Chi Minh.

Chuck Wallace, a black friend in seventh grade, told me he'd see I was treated well after the Black Panthers seized control of the country. I told him our society wasn't going over just yet. But, honestly, who knew?

[*three*]

Supermen
need not apply

THE SEARCH FOR ANSWERS WAS ON. PEOPLE started looking for the answers everywhere. San Francisco, India, Tibet. Pot, acid, LSD.

Me, I wasn't much for travel or drugs. I was by then in my teens, thoughtful and grasping for answers. So I started to read.

Most of my teachers (many of whom had gone into education to avoid the draft) were left wing politically. Under their guidance I began reading the tracts of the left: *Das Kapital, The Manifesto, The Little Red Book.* Guess what? It was all nonsense. Kill all the rich guys. Then set up a dictatorship of the proletariat. Now all the little guys slave for you, while you live in the rich guy's house and tell the starving peasants about social justice.

Then I read the stuff from the right: Nietzsche, Smith, Rand. This was a little better, but flawed as well. Sure, it was great if you were a superman like Howard Roark or John Galt. I mean, who could be against building skyscrapers and partying all night? But what if you were crippled, retarded or sick? What kind of value system could it be if it had no place for those who really needed help? No wonder everyone was going to India. A lot of people thought they would find a better alternative in Eastern thought.

Not that I wasn't coming onto some authentic truths, ones that resonated with my innate values. The deepest one was probably the Jeffersonian idea of Natural Rights—that we are all born with a certain inalienable natural freedom. That it is wrong to take this freedom from us, and that the *only* excuse for limiting this freedom is protecting others' rights. Thus, you should be free to do whatever you'd like with your own life, provided your actions don't end up hurting, killing or stealing from others. What a great idea! We're not just objects or vassals. Each human being is something holy—almost G-d-like, with his or her own natural rights.

The notion first put forth by the 18th century economist Adam Smith, that if people are allowed to act economically in their own self-interest, the most goods would be produced and the largest number of people's needs satisfied, was also a tremendous idea. It fit wonderfully with the concept of natural rights. If people were not only politically free, but economically free as well, everyone would be better off. Now here was a set of ideas I could really identify with.

Could such an ideal work in practice? Was it possible to set up a society where eventually someone wouldn't seize control of the central power and take away everyone else's freedom? John Locke, the 17th century British philosopher, proposed the idea of the balance of powers, which seemed to answer this problem. What if from the outset a government were set up separating the powers to make and to enforce laws, and separating the power to levy taxes from the power to spend? What if an independent judiciary existed which could judge disputes between the legislative and the executive powers? What if all this could be done within a framework that guaranteed the political and economic rights of everyone in that society, using an unshackled press to monitor any abuse of these rights? Well, that libertarian ideal would be an *almost* perfect society. Almost—except for the orphans, the disabled, the helpless and those without any hope or prospects. What about them?

The problem with libertarian dogma was the problem with all dogma, whether of the left or the right. If you try to build your whole value system around a single principle, be it equality, ethnic unity or even freedom, that system eventually demands that reason and decency be sacrificed in the name of the higher principle. Examples of this abound. The liberty of the Roman republic gave rise to debauchery, corruption and trading in human beings, as the elite went about satisfying their own desires without consideration for the less fortunate. The fraternity of the French revolution quickly led even its most fervent stalwarts to the guillotine. And the equality promised by Communists like Stalin and Mao led tens of millions to death, imprisonment or, for the lucky, near starvation.

If a social system built on principle, just like systems based on arbitrary power, inexorably results in abuse and misery, is humanity just destined for misery? Was the Camelot ideal—which seemed to die with John F. Kennedy—really impossible after all? For my own part, I decided I'd just be a nice libertarian, one who worked hard but gave charity. No one, I thought, was ever going to come up with a perfect system.

Then one day I picked up a Bible* and started reading. I was amazed. There it all was—the libertarian ideal. Abraham refused to bury his wife Sarah until he was allowed to purchase a burial place that would belong to his family eternally—an example of property rights. There are more examples of property rights—thou shalt not steal, thou shalt not even covet thy neighbor's property (with the hope of stealing it). Neither thou nor the king. Thy vineyard is thy vineyard and thy house is thy house. And

---

*When I say "Bible," I'm generally referring to the first major chunk of it, also known as the Five Books of Moses, the Pentateuch (in Greek), or the Torah (in Hebrew). For simplicity's sake, I'll just call it the Bible.

nobody better abuse thy person either. Thou shalt not murder. Thou best not assault because thou shalt surely pay—an eye for an eye, a tooth for a tooth (but not literally)*. No kidnapping either. Death for that. So much for the crime problem.

And just because you're rich or in the government doesn't mean that you have the right to step on anyone else. The king isn't even allowed to have too many horses or too many wives. And the courts are expressly forbidden to give any special treatment to the rich. Don't try the sympathy angle, though; they're forbidden to give special consideration to the poor as well. Justice, justice shall you pursue. Now that's really neat, I thought.

Even the separation of powers was built in. You had the king, the High Priest, and the courts. There was sometimes a prophet, as well, to unmask wrongdoing and keep everyone on his toes. Later came the Sanhedrin (the Supreme Court), which served as a rule-

---

*Jewish law always understood these verses to refer to monetary compensation.

making body and the court of final appeal.

The king had some obligations I found especially interesting. First, he had to copy by hand the entire Bible using a quill on heavy parchment, a lengthy and difficult task. Then he had to carry this spiritual document of liberty with him wherever he went. And, periodically, he had to assemble the citizenry and read to them from the Bible so everyone would know just what their rights and obligations were.

What an incredible way to see the king internalize these values! Isn't the internal value system of the executive the only ultimate check against the most extreme abuses of the balance of power? Wouldn't it have been anathema even for a president like Nixon, raised on the doctrines of the Bill of Rights and the rest of the American Constitution, to have fomented a crisis and seize emergency military authority to hold onto power during Watergate? Isn't this the reason that an American president swears to protect, honor and defend the Constitution of the United States at his inauguration?

Yeah, the Bible was certainly the libertarian

ideal. No wonder the Founding Fathers of the United States nearly decided to make Hebrew rather than English the national language of this nation of liberty.

But it was the Bible's exceptions to libertarian principle that struck me even more forcefully than the Bible's adoption of libertarian principle itself. Farmers were commanded to leave a corner of their field unharvested for the poor. Every Jew was ethically obligated to donate at least ten percent of his income. Lenders were not permitted to charge interest on their loans. Even the largest debts were discharged every seven years.

But there was one law that blew me away and made me into an observant Jew. At the age of seventeen, this one law literally made me change my life, simply because, once I discovered it, I had to concede that the Bible was the work of Divine genius.

Once every fifty years, in what is known as the *Yovel* (jubilee) year, all farmland (that is, the means of production in an agrarian society) must revert to its original owner's family. This meant that no matter how destitute or without hope a person might be, once every fifty years—at least once in the average lifetime—that person would have the means of production, the opportunity to rise to any level, placed back in his own hands. It took over 3,000 years for ideas like that to resurface in the form of the Homestead Act (which, in 1862, allowed anyone to claim land as theirs if they had worked it or lived there for at least five years), the GI Bill (which, beginning in 1944, provided education and training for millions of veterans) and, of course, public education (which provides free education to all children).

But this Biblical law of the jubilee year guaranteed opportunity to every member of society. It wasn't just a redistribution of wealth, because gold, art, houses, even palatial residences in walled cities didn't revert. It was the *opportunity* that the land represented for independence, self-sufficiency and self-betterment that was redistributed. Prices of such land were always calculated taking this fifty-year cycle into account.

In this jubilee year, the ram's horn would be sounded and liberty would be proclaimed to all the inhabitants of the land therein. Do you know where these inspiring words are inscribed today? On the Liberty Bell, in Philadelphia. Makes you think, huh?

[four]

I *got the power*!

IT SURE MADE ME THINK. WHEN I DISCOVERED these Biblical laws, I was simply astonished. What a perfect compromise between pure laisséz faire economics and wealth redistribution strategies, which just lead to a welfare-state cycle of dependence.

But who was it who had thought of all this? Could it be Divine wisdom? Or maybe, to be more precise, a Divine decree?

The Bible, I discovered, is not a book of advice. It's a book of laws. The ancient Israelites were governed by and had to obey the dictums of the Bible (as is true for Jews today). So how did these laws originate? Who wrote them and put them into force? There were only two possibilities—G-d or man.

The problem with the human explanation is that people only do things that are in their own self-interest. The laws that people write are always created to serve the particular interest of the person or party with the power to institute the laws.

Take me, for example. I'm the founder and chairman of a large telecommunications company called IDT. We're a public company and my stock is worth a substantial amount of money. But guess what? I don't own a majority of the stock. Long ago I had to sell my majority stake to thousands of individual investors and large mutual funds, who now own the majority of our equity. But guess what else? At every annual shareholder's meeting, I personally control the majority of the votes and decide all-important matters of policy. True, in the last several years our revenue, stock price and profits have consistently increased, so currently almost all the investors happily give me their proxies each year. But even were I to totally mismanage things and drive us to the brink of bankruptcy, I'd still control the majority of the votes. Know why? Because I have super-voting stock. Every one of my shares gets three votes and everyone else gets only one. Is this fair? No. But that's how it is. Know why? Because the person who had the power, when the bylaws were written, set it up that way. That person let the prospective investors know in advance that if they wanted to buy shares in IDT, they'd have to do it accepting that condition, otherwise they could invest in some other company. Naturally, no one liked the condition, but they had no choice. The guy who wrote the bylaws had all the power. Now let me ask you a question. Who do you think that guy was?

Mea culpa. I admit it. I had the power and I intended to keep it. And I'm not sorry. Come what may, I don't have to worry. The market can go up or down. This book may sell or die on the shelves. I'm not worried. I know I'll have a job next year. I've got a lifetime contract. I wrote it myself.

In this regard, I am like the railroad barons who controlled the state legislatures in order to secure rights of way through public lands, like the ancient conquerors who had themselves crowned kings, like the revolutionary Russian Communists who put their party in charge of everything when they took over, or like the independent farmers and tradesmen who threw the British out and vested power in the hands of the people in America.

The rule is simple—laws are put into force by those in power and are enacted for their own benefit. Who, then, came up with the idea that for fifty years the wealthy could pile up as much wealth and power as they desired, but that at the end of fifty years they had to return any land they had acquired? Was it the wealthy? Obviously not. The poor, then? No way. Why wait fifty years if they had the power? Why only the farmland? Who, then, could possibly have come up with this stuff?

More questions come to mind. Who invented the idea of leaving the corner of one's field unharvested and giving away ten percent of what is harvested? The rich? No way, they'd want to keep it all. The poor? Why only ten percent then?

What about the law that prohibits judges from showing favoritism to either the rich or the poor? Which side, I ask you, pressed for that? In fact, the more I looked into these questions, the more I was mystified.

The priestly clan was a possible suspect, since "taxes" supporting them were institutionalized. But if this group "wrote" the Bible, then why did they exclude themselves from the distribution of land or deny themselves the ability to marry whomever they wished?

If the king "wrote" the Bible, why would he forbid himself from having too many wives or horses? Why would he agree to submit to the law in so many cases? Where was the Divine Right of kings?

If neither the rich nor the poor were the beneficiaries, then who came up with all these laws, which were so just yet favored no one?

Which tribal society more than 3,000 years ago would have ever come up on their own with a law that affords full legal protection and rights to any foreigner who wandered onto their territory?

Foreigners at that time (and in many parts of the world even now) were subject to enslavement, robbing, raping or killing. Who came up with the idea of respecting the rights of the sojourner and doing him or her no harm because you and your ancestors were sojourners in Egypt? Wouldn't exacting revenge on Egyptians and other foreigners have had a lot more popular appeal? (It sure seems to today!) The Hutu, the Tutsi, Blacks who've wandered into a Ku Klux Klan neighborhood, Greeks in Turkey, Turks in Greece. These groups can all attest to whole heaps of abuse. And yet, here it was. This was the Bible. The Law. G-d's law.

And then it hit me. The undeniable reality. The Bible really was G-d's revealed law. It was the source of all morality in the world. G-d planted the seed and gave us this Tree of Life, this source of morality. And then humanity spent most of its history ignoring it and doing what came naturally. But I decided then and there, while still a teenager, that I could no longer ignore it, and I became religiously observant.

Eventually I came to see that the seed of morality never really died. Carried by the Jews and partially transplanted into other world religions, it kept sprouting and asserting itself again and again, like the stalk that grows through concrete. It kept coming back, refusing to die, again and again confronting power with morality.

Is it then really any wonder that those who opposed this morality were most intent on wiping out the Jews, the historical custodians of this moral truth? Just think of Hitler, Stalin and, two thousand years earlier, the Roman general Titus—all of whom declared themselves G-d and tried to force the world to accept their edicts as the new morality.

Is it any wonder either that the United States was founded by Christians fleeing oppression, inspired by the Old Testament, who began their Declaration of Independence with the words: "We hold these Truths to be self-evident, that all Men are created equal, that they are endowed *by their Creator** with certain *unalienable Rights*, that among these are Life, Liberty and the Pursuit of Happiness"?

Is it any wonder that the United States was founded on the dream of opportunity within the principles of economic and political liberty? Is it any wonder that the United States not only

*emphasis is that of the author

extends full legal rights to sojourners, but in fact is a nation of immigrants?

Is it any wonder that the United States too has found itself again and again confronting many of the very same villains who declare themselves to be G-d? I think not.

Yet, even though suppressed for centuries, the truth in the Bible has not only refused to be squelched but has spread. So too American values, almost universally vilified by regimes around the world, have continued to spread through movies, music, jeans and even the Internet, while once dominant regimes like the Soviet Union have simply collapsed before a stronger set of values, and the Berlin Wall, much like its counterpart in Jericho, has come tumbling down.

Does this give me reason for optimism? You bet. But as the Bible warns, freedom comes with obligations. Prosperity demands careful adherence to the morality that the Bible encourages. It is my hope that the realization that this morality is in fact Divine will encourage people to pay it greater heed.

[five]

Peanut butter
and jelly

THE BIBLE IS G-D'S REVEALED LAW AND THE source of all morality. While there's certainly a lot we don't understand about G-d, much of what we can appreciate about G-d we learn from the perfection of the Bible. We can actually glimpse the righteousness and goodness of G-d by coming to appreciate the morality and fairness inherent in the Bible.

It seems to me that each person has to decide what kind of god he or she wants to believe in. I believe that a god of less than perfect morality and fairness, a god without the Bible, could not be G-d. It would be just a power, comparable to any other power in the world. The fact that a being possesses power is not a reason to worship it. Power can be used for evil. I suppose that some people could believe in an evil god, but I cannot. As I see it, *defying* an evil god would be better and more G-dly, if you will, than worshiping such a god.

Fortunately, the good found in the universe —the greater productivity of free men and the ultimate triumphs of good over evil—*prove* that G-d is in fact not evil.

People are sometimes tempted to ask, if G-d is so good, how come He allows bad things to happen to good people? For that matter, how come He lets bad things happen to *any* people, good or bad?

First, let's put things in perspective. This morning, in the university cafeteria where I like to write, I had a delicious cup of espresso, a scrumptious bagel and some really good fresh orange juice. All this, while sitting in my favorite chair, across from my wife Debbie, my favorite person, preparing to pontificate on my version of absolute truth (one of my favorite activities). Had the cafeteria guy given me tea, rye bread and grapefruit juice, rather than my favorites, I'd have been less than delighted. Were my chair broken or my wife busy, I might not even be writing this. But no, everything was exactly the way I wanted it. From all the billions and billions of possible circumstances I could have been in, I was in exactly the situation I chose. And you know what? So are the vast majority of people.

It reminds me of an old story. Two Italian construction workers, Anthony and Salvatore, are sitting on a girder, forty floors above Madison Avenue, about to have lunch. Salvatore opens his lunch box and extracts a gorgeous looking meatball hero, still warm and oozing thick tomato sauce.

"Ah, a meatball hero," he sighs contentedly. Then with both hands he takes a big bite, chews, takes a swig of Coke and exclaims, "That's good!"

Anthony watches all this, then reaches into his own lunch box and extracts a small white bread sandwich. He lifts the corners, grimaces and says, "Ech, peanut butter and jelly."

The next day Anthony and Salvatore sit down again for lunch on the girder and this time Salvatore extracts a hero even more regal than that of the previous day, with not only sauce but melted mozzarella cheese almost gushing out. He has to squeeze the sandwich to get it between his lips and closes his eyes in sheer delight as he swallows and murmurs, "What an eggplant parmigiana hero!"

Tony watches all this, reaches into his own lunchbox, extracts a small square of wax paper, unwraps it, lifts the white bread and exclaims in even greater disgust, "Oh no, peanut butter and jelly again!"

The third day back on the girder, Sal pulls out of his lunchbox a roast beef hero, one Verdi could write an opera over. Succulent roast beef pops out from every angle. The sandwich is dripping with mustard and mayonnaise and bursting with sautéed onions. Sal takes one bite and experiences such ecstasy that, if not for years of experience on the girders, he might have dropped forty stories to culinary heaven. "Mama Mia," Sal almost prays, "that's good!"

Tony reaches into his own box and takes out, once again, the hated peanut butter and jelly sandwich. He takes one look at the sandwich, flings it forty stories down and begins to sob.

Sal tries to comfort him. "Tony, if you don't like peanut butter and jelly, why don't you tell your wife not to make it every day?"

"What wife?" Tony responds. "I make my own lunch."

The reason you might laugh is that more than a few of us are like Tony. Most of us get exactly the lunch we want, because that's what we choose to eat.

It may be an unpleasant reality to face, but much of the evil in this world is self-inflicted. Millions of people are smoking themselves into lung cancer, eating themselves into heart disease, and drinking themselves into liver disease. They're beating their spouses into divorce, stealing themselves into jail and racing their ways into accidents. Bars are more populated than gyms. Video stores are busier than libraries. Yet, when the inevitable occurs, people usually fault G-d for cancer, divorce, car accidents and spiritual estrangement. Ah, well.

Consider this, though: On the roads and highways of the world, people encounter millions of other cars—two-ton, three-hundred-horsepower missiles of death—many of which are piloted by individuals who are distressed, inebriated or—even worse—driving with kids in the back seat. Miraculously, though, almost all these millions of individuals get where they're going. True, we tend to focus on the accidents, and on the famines and floods, but isn't the fact that billions of people are *not* starving, that the vast majority of people are *not* living amidst natural destruction, and that we confidently hop into cars and get where we're going the true miracle?

Basically, the processes of the world, the changing of the seasons, plants bearing fruit, love and birth, are good. The fact that cuts heal, sadness diminishes with time, and effort overcomes need, is good.

In fact, against all odds, good usually triumphs in this world. Penicillin has overcome infection. Vaccines have vanquished polio.

For every new disease like AIDS, dozens of other diseases have been cured.

Even more outstanding is the triumph of good in relations among people. Realistically, doesn't it seem that, if might makes right, the Hitlers, Stalins and Husseins of the world ought to rule over everyone? Logically, should a nation of free people making movies and preparing cappuccinos be a military match for societies devoted to militarism and world domination? On first glance, no—no more than a few accounting students walking home from school should be a match for a youth gang. And think what values we'd all have, had Hitler or Stalin actually achieved world domination. Would anyone even know who G-d was or what the Bible was? Yet, the truly evil, despite their strengths and initial successes, and against all odds, have never achieved the total domination necessary to wipe out G-d's message.

[six]

Caffé lattes win the day

OR WAS IT AGAINST THE ODDS? WHY HAS EVIL failed to achieve world domination? Has G-d built a mechanism into human affairs that accounts for the inevitable triumph of good over evil? I think so.

The mechanism, I think, is to be found in the differences between free economies and societies, and ones that are controlled. Freedom and individual rights, as I've said, are what I believe to be at the heart of G-d's value system. To allow people freedom is good. To enslave them is bad. That's one reason why G-d gave the Israelites the Bible after He led them out of bondage in Egypt to freedom. Only after seeing the difference between bondage and freedom could the Israelites appreciate the difference between good and evil. And, in fact, among the first commands to the Jews is the command to celebrate their redemption from slavery every year.

Practically, controlled societies simply are not as productive as free societies. Their workers, lacking the profit motive, are not as motivated. Their managers, unable to use supply and demand to price commodities and allocate resources, eventually fail utterly in coordinating all the elements of an economic system, and production inevitably grinds to a halt. Interestingly, it usually takes time for this to happen. In the beginning, controlled societies tend to be highly successful at building steel foundries and munitions plants. They just forcibly relocate workers, redirect trains, reallocate resources and, *voila*, steel and bombs appear in great numbers. But almost as soon as they get done patting themselves on the back, the trouble begins.

There are no pens to keep track of production because the pen factory's conveyor belt was moved to the steel foundry. There is not enough food for the workers because the food factory's key employees are all in the munitions plants. The electricity keeps going out and delaying production because almost all the crude oil has been used to make petrochemicals for weapons production, leaving the local power plant dry. Not to worry. The tyrant bureaucrat just redirects more assets to solve the problem and, of course, the situation gets even worse, until the whole economy virtually shuts down.

Soon the brazen, once-victorious, frontline troops of the fatherland have neither adequate weapons nor fuel nor food, let alone new technology, and the tide of battle changes.

The cappuccino makers, film moguls and accountants from the free society, driven by the profit motive, set up munitions plants that truly work. Espresso roasters are converted to smelters where the profit is greater. Movie producers start looking for oil to supply the plants. Accountants make sure everything is profitable and arrives on schedule. Suddenly the arsenal of democracy is booming. Formerly apathetic young people rush to enlist as their society is truly threatened. Even the strange birds and odd ducks, which a society that values individualism tends to spawn, start breaking the enemy's codes and inventing new technologies.

Suddenly, the fascist or communist regime is outgunned and outmanned. Its forces lose heart and begin to retreat. Having only compulsion on which to rely, the authorities start arbitrarily shooting and imprisoning almost everyone. Officers, soldiers, bureaucrats, workers, everyone is in danger and soon everyone is hoping to lose, wanting to surrender, just to free themselves of the controlling regime. (Certainly, the Germans and Japanese lived better under the American occupation that followed World War II than they had under their own rulers).

Against all odds, the accountants, dock workers and auto workers from the free world parade through the enemy capital in triumph. Against all odds, the individualistic society has licked the controlled society. Later, against all odds, the more individualistic American society would use the speed of change and innovation wrought by computers and the Internet to lick the seemingly infallible but more collectivist Japanese economic empire. In the end, G-d set the world up in such a way that good always triumphs.

He didn't have to. He could have had capitalism not work. He could have made it so that the society with the strongest central leader was the strongest society. But I think that would have been inconsistent with a G-d whose central value is liberty.

seven

No one robs Fort Knox

NOW ON TO THE REALLY BIG QUESTION—THE terrible things that happen to people for which they truly are not to blame, things that happen to those who really didn't make their own luck.

As I've pointed out, the main thing G-d wants is for people to be free—free to make their own choices, free to create, free to achieve, free to remember, free to choose good over evil, free to create good things which will overcome hardship and misery, free to remember one's values and one's origins even when overwhelmed by the excitement or temptation of the moment, free to love even to the point of self-sacrifice. To be able to do these things is what makes one really human. It makes one almost like G-d, which is what the Bible says is the whole point. But in order to achieve this level, both evil and free choice must exist.

From the earliest time, G-d has ordered us to subdue the physical world (see Genesis 1:28), to overcome weather conditions by building houses and making clothes, to overcome starvation by planting fields and thirst by digging wells. Are heat and cold evil because we would bake or freeze without shelter and garments? Of course not, though many men have died of frostbite or heatstroke. Is it evil when wheat does not just grow freely without being planted or that in many places fresh water can only be found by sinking wells? Obviously not. Though millions have died of starvation or dehydration for lack of such wells or crops, the glory of man is in overcoming such obstacles.

If we were able to eat and drink and be protected from the elements without effort, we'd just be parasites on the planet. No one would work. No one would achieve anything. No one would be admired or have any accomplishments of which to be proud. We'd be worth little more than the fruits that would spontaneously drop from trees into our mouths.

G-d gave us a world where natural forces

are regenerating and adaptive. One species of plant replaces another to regenerate the forest after a fire or damage caused by a man-made hydrocarbon. Do these same natural forces sometimes cause cancer, hardening of the arteries and strokes? Certainly, but they can also be used to cure them.

We were not intended to live forever in this world. The goal of life is to go through the whole life cycle, to be born, grow, learn, love, have children, pass on values to the next generation, and then leave, making room for the next generation to make their own mark.

Would this be accomplished if people were immortal? Would any politician have a chance if a vigorous George Washington still occupied the White House, or would any businessman be able to compete against a dynamic Rockefeller who has endless years to consolidate his position? Would there be any real freedom if the powerful, granted immortality, attempted to find ways to hold their superior positions forever? I think not. It is the natural way for a son to assume leadership of the family from his father or a daughter from her mother. That people are not immortal is not evil but good. That's what being human is all about.

Tragedies, natural or otherwise, are to be dealt with or overcome and, if possible, prevented. They come with the natural world and, fortunately, they occur rarely.

The biggest question people ask, though, is not why bad things happen, but why they happen to good people. This is actually a much simpler problem.

Once again, it helps to remember that the most important thing, from G-d's point of view, is that people are free, that they have free choice. In fact, the very thing that defines "good people" is their exercise of free choice to do good, often through self-sacrifice. If every decision they made were in their own interest, they wouldn't be good or human at all. They'd be just like a plant, which always seeks out the light, irrespective of the effect on other plants. Or like an animal, which goes after food or follows its mating instinct, irrespective of whether other animals are starving or interested.

Free choice implies that sometimes doing that which you know to be right will in fact be painful, harmful or at least not as pleasurable, remunerative or rewarding as doing that which you know to be wrong. Only in the spiritual sense, in the sense that doing right always gives you the moral satisfaction of knowing you did good, is righteousness always rewarded.

If evil people were always punished for their immoral choices, they would simply not choose the immoral. Were all wives the most desirable women in their husbands' eyes, and all other casual or not-so-casual female acquaintances utterly unappealing, there would be no need for the commandment against adultery (at least from the male point of view). There would be no choice. Similarly, were all immorally amassed wealth automatically rendered worthless, we wouldn't need the commandment against stealing. No sane person would bother.

Obviously, then, by definition, it is at least sometimes necessary for the good to suffer and the wicked to thrive. Anything less would eliminate choice. In an even larger sense, the

Ultimate Power in the universe and the Supreme Advocate for good must hide Himself in order to preserve free choice. He must make His existence a matter of speculation and faith. Were His existence and power to be manifest and obvious, free choice would be eliminated, as surely as a police car standing at the corner eliminates the temptation to run a red light.

No one robs Fort Knox because an army garrison guards it. No one steals towels from a hotel when the manager is in the room. No one insults his heart surgeon prior to an operation for fear the scalpel may "slip." Everyone acts courteously to a prospective employer, respect-fully when meeting their prospective in-laws, and religiously when their clergyman is around. These situations eliminate a person's free choice.

How much more so would free choice be eliminated if people knew for sure that G-d was always watching, and that even the smallest of their acts would be punished or rewarded, as appropriate. Were this the case, everyone would always do good. No one would ever do evil, and all free choice would be eliminated.

This is exactly what would happen. If bad things never happened to good people, neither those who were charitable nor their children would ever contract cancer. Soon an absolute link would be found between those who gave to the United Way and those who never got cancer, and everyone would give, *not* out of their own free choice to help others, but just to avoid disease. It would be discovered that no one who coached little league or served as a scoutmaster ever lost money in a stock deal. People would be waking up at two in the morning, beating other would-be coaches with baseball bats, and tying up fellow would-be scoutmasters with square knots just to be first in line to be selected as a coach or adviser—not because they wanted to do good, but because they wanted the reward. They'd have no choice. If none of the children of the righteous ever died in car accidents or in war, everyone would act righteously, not out of altruism but out of fear.

For this reason, G-d must let bad things happen to good people. In this otherwise basically benevolent world, He must let the natural processes go forward, allowing the wicked to thrive, often at the expense of the righteous, until the natural laws of the universe bring them down, as all the wicked eventually fall.

By giving the wicked the ability to succeed, G-d also gives good people the opportunity to overcome evil—to fight for good by making the sacrifices required when faced with evil. This is how, if all goes well, evil is again and again expunged from the world.

[eight]

Course corrections

OCCASIONALLY, THOUGH, THE GOOD ARE TOO FEW, too weak or too oppressed and leaderless to oppose evil. Then the world goes through terrible periods. Even in these periods, though, G-d has not forgotten humanity. In fact, it is in these times, like during the Holocaust, for instance, that G-d is most active.

Aboard the ship that is the world, all hell may be breaking loose. Passengers may be killing each other, and the boat may be rocking to such an extent that it seems like it will go under. The destination seems like it will never be reached.

It is only at this time, after the fact, when man has exercised his free will in the face of the worst, when the ship is clearly going off course, when all seems lost, that G-d steps in. Then the sea begins to do funny things. It throws the ship first this way, then that, inexplicably tossing everyone about, some even off the ship. Evil people die, heroes are born. Alliances and behavior patterns change. Good asserts itself again, and strong currents cause the ship to suddenly, miraculously emerge from the storm back on the right course and in calm waters again. Free choice on the boat was never eliminated, but heaven made a course correction nevertheless.

Look at the Holocaust and the events of World War II as an example. Hitler and the Nazis, with victory virtually assured, inexplicably turned not against the almost defenseless British but against Stalin, their partner in evil. With this, the Nazis doomed themselves. They allowed America, the citadel of democracy, time to re-supply Britain and build up its own forces while the Germans froze at Stalingrad in the Russian winter.

Look at Hitler's war on the Jews. Every nation shut its door to the Jewish people, who were thus condemned to die in the Holocaust. Then G-d—seeing that no nation could be trusted to protect the keepers of His Covenant—almost miraculously allowed the State of Israel to be born, providing true refuge to the Jews. The Jews, who for millennia were defenseless against Cossacks, Crusaders or Nazis, were finally granted some measure of protection. Ironically, it was a Jewish scientist escaping from the Nazis who gave America the ability to create the atomic bomb, which guaranteed an allied victory in World War II. Is G-d's hand really so hard to see in the corrective currents following evil's temporary successes?

Speaking of miracles, I must mention the collapse of the Soviet Union. Sure, the superiority of the free economic system in the West made it inevitable that it would eventually go under. But let's just take a second to consider this. These people possessed the world's second largest nuclear arsenal, an arsenal capable of destroying the world many times over. Many strong tyrants have been overthrown in history, but never without bloody battles. Never have they succumbed without first exhausting their military might and making the world pay in blood. Further, never has the power that evil possessed been so formidable that just a fraction of it could destroy humanity.

People ask, where was G-d when the oppressive Soviet regime acquired the power to annihilate mankind? Yet, to some extent, terrible things are fixable. The fact that we're still here to even ask the question speaks to this fact. Had those bombs gone off, there would have been no questions. There would have been no opportunity for fixing the problem later. Mankind would have been wiped out, and the planet uninhabitable. And yet, what happened to the Russian monster, the Communist empire, the Great Bear? It simply called it a day. It laid down its weapons, and the world's largest, most repressive army just went home and applied for unemployment insurance.

And people ask, where was G-d? Whenever the challenges are too enormous, He's there.

nine

Scoring despite a strong defense

WHILE G-D'S HAND CAN BE SEEN IN THE FACE OF impending disaster, such as in single-handedly preventing thermonuclear war, the difficulties we face as individuals are of a different degree. Not losing one's temper, grace in the face of adversity, confronting an unpleasant medical reality—these are the challenges we're confronted with every day.

And thank G-d we are. If there were no challenges, life would be boring. It would be like playing miniature golf on a course where a deep groove went directly from the tee to the hole. Every shot would be a hole in one, no windmills to stop the ball, no phony duck ponds for it to fall into, just one hole in one after another. After a week or so you could just close the course. No one would be interested in playing.

The fact is, people like to be challenged.

That's why there are handicaps in golf, why a baseball is so hard to hit, why the linebacker's job is to take the quarterback before he can throw. Anyone can score touchdown after touchdown if there are no defenders. The satisfaction comes with scoring *against* a strong defense.

Similarly, in life the goal is to confront challenges and, if possible, overcome them. If not, at least there's the satisfaction of having tried or having done your best. This is what life is about. It's what makes us human.

In the Bible, we see that Abraham was confronted by G-d with ten tests. Did you ever wonder, why did G-d bother? Didn't G-d know this was a good guy? I mean, He picked *him* out from all humanity as the main man.

The truth is, G-d, Who knows everything, knew Abraham would emerge from the furnace unscathed and He knew Abraham would be willing to sacrifice his son and heir Isaac as G-d asked. But confronting the challenges, taking the tests, made Abraham a better person.

It turns out that people who've lived

through adversity and confronted challenges are deeper people than those who haven't. It's that simple.

Want to have a meaningless conversation? Just find some rich kid in a fancy car outside a singles bar in some wealthy suburb and start talking about the meaning of life. Then try it again with somebody just back from a couple of years in the Peace Corps or returning from visiting a sick relative, or better yet, returning from a hospital stay of their own. Tell me which set of experiences builds character.

It's not our job, though, to sit around waiting to be hospitalized or drafted, any more than it's our job to hang around waiting to be hit by lightning. If major challenges were constantly thrust upon us, we wouldn't necessarily grow from them. Instead, we would be more likely to develop the umbrella reflex—insulating ourselves from all challenges, the way people instantly open their umbrellas at the first sight of rain.

The real idea is to challenge oneself every day, to try to live life to the fullest and become a bigger person by attempting to climb new mountains. Someone who lives this way, when challenges *are* thrust upon him, will be well prepared.

ten

Sweeping your way to the top

NOT EVERY CHALLENGE FACED WILL RESULT IN success. Sometimes, the golf ball will hit the windmill or land in the pond. This is the nature of life. In fact, the more one tries, the more windmills one will hit. Yet people often look at successful people and think, "Wow, what a charmed life that guy has."

I don't see it that way. Financially and personally, I've had enormous success. And yet, I've had more than my fair share of failures. Not only that, but every success has come with responsibility: more employees whose jobs I'm responsible for, more investors risking their money on me, more charities I'm being asked to support.

When I see successful people, I usually see the responsibilities lining their faces, memories of failure tempering their rise, a certain determination to move forward preceding their movements. Are these people happier than their more carefree counterparts? I don't think so. Success is not a reward. Sometimes it's just a sign of having tried hard and often.

There is, in my opinion, a sort of brotherhood of achievers, which transcends all physical and financial boundaries. I perceive three classes of people in the world: shirkers who go through life trying to mooch off the efforts of others, regular people who do what's expected of them but nothing extra, and those who go all out to try to accomplish the most they can with whatever G-d gave them. Measure for measure, G-d often grants these truly G-dly people tremendous success, and they are the ones who tend to drive society forward.

Some of these achievers may be corporate CEOs or top athletes. Others may be janitors. But the janitors amongst the group run the cleanest, friendliest buildings anyone's ever seen. And it shows. So how is it that they're not eventually promoted for their efforts?

When I was a little boy, my father, a self-made achiever but not a religiously inclined person, told me a story—I have no idea where he heard it—that always stayed with me. It was the story of how Joseph, a slave in Egypt, rose to be master of Potiphar's house.

Potiphar was the prime minister of Egypt, the world's most powerful country at the time. He had hundreds, perhaps even thousands, of servants. All the servants, however, had a servant mentality. Just do the assigned task as quickly as possible and go on an all-day lunch break while Potiphar is away at the ministry with Pharaoh.

Joseph, a lowly Hebrew slave, had one of the simplest jobs in the household, just to sweep the floor. Joseph, though, had something special in him. Taking a break when more work could be done didn't seem right. Not only that, but the floors could always use another sweeping, then another, then one more. One day, Potiphar showed up particularly late and all the other servants had left, all except Joseph. He was still sweeping the floor just one more time, and by then it shined. Potiphar realized that here was a man he could trust. For if this slave wouldn't even "steal" a moment's rest from him, how much more so would not he steal from his household.

Joseph not only rose to be master of Potiphar's house, but wouldn't even "steal" Potiphar's beautiful wife when she threw herself at him. Eventually—after several "hiccups" along the way—this led to Joseph's becoming Viceroy of all Egypt and the savior of his people. Why? Because he kept on sweeping.

This story had a dramatic effect on my life. I started as a hot dog vendor, moved on to drive a delivery truck, and have wound up owning an international telecommunications firm and another company with a dozen trade publications. Why? Partly talent. Partly luck. But also because I made sure my hot dogs were the best and I made sure I kept delivering late at night after all the other delivery guys were sleeping.

I've kept this Joseph story in mind as I've built my company. I've never insisted on hiring the guys from the best schools or with the fanciest resumes. I've always wanted the people with a fire burning in them. The ones who would sweep the floors a thousand times if left alone. A lot of these people—many of whom might still be "sweeping" somewhere else—are controlling or building much of the telecommunications infrastructure at IDT.

The point is, I feel there's much more in common between a disabled person pushing himself to succeed in the Special Olympics and a Michael Jordan or a Bill Gates, than there is between the super-achievers and those just going through the motions. All people are brothers and sisters. All people have G-d within them. But the people who not only accept but embrace life's challenges, no matter what their objective level of accomplishment—these people are truly actualizing G-d's will for humanity.

The charities that have the most appeal for me are those that give people the chance to elevate themselves: libraries, vocational reha-bilitation, schools, and refugee and immigrant assistance. Sure, soup kitchens are wonderful and need to be supported, but cooking schools are better. Those who graduate can make their own soup.

eleven

Hitting bottom

FAILURE AND HARDSHIP ARE PART OF THE HUMAN condition. As the old cliché reminds us, into every life rain falls. Sometimes it just sprinkles and the car won't start, the kids fight, the client cancels or a raise doesn't come through. Other times it's a literal downpour as we face death, disease, divorce, debt and depression. (Ever notice how many bad things start with D?)

People who have faith can turn to their faith to get them through. People who understand that the nature of life is to have ups and downs can accept the downs when they arrive. Those who've fearfully spent life avoiding challenges and risks are more often than not knocked senseless when life's inevitable challenges come a-knocking. People who are willing to confront challenge may have faced failure, but the failure has often been on their own terms and at their own initiative, thus easier to deal with. Risk-takers who parachute from planes and ride roller coasters are comparatively less fearful when their commercial airliner goes through turbulence.

Simply stated, people who confront challenges are aware that there are ups and downs and neither one is forever. This makes it easier for them to deal with both. Although I can't deny I'm wealthy, this knowledge, surprisingly enough, has made it impossible for me to give up my middle-class lifestyle. Why get used to something that is potentially impermanent? Why give up a perfectly good set of values and friends just to join a "better" club, which would never want you as a member *without* your bank account? It's better to hang out with the hot dog vendors, the delivery drivers, even corporate chieftains who acknowledge each other's value and G-dliness and the effort they put into trying, than join a group that worships only the fruits of those efforts.

It is how we deal with the aftermath of failure and hardship that truly defines us. G-d could have put us in a "perfect" world, a world where nothing goes wrong and there are no wrongs to right. But He chose to put us in this world so we, as G-d's partners, could make it better, so we could be like G-d and create our own goodness and perfection.

When a sick child is born, the G-dly thing to do is not to doubt G-d's kindness but to help care for and, if possible, raise the child. The proper response to famine is not questioning but feeding. When confronting yet another tragedy, we should respond not with hopelessness but with love. This brings G-d into the world. Every hardship must somehow be seen as an opportunity for elevation.

The truth is, when I'm confronted with the terrible suffering of terminally ill people, I sometimes sympathize in my heart with the desire of some people in this situation to end their lives. What is the point of life when *all* it contains is acute physical suffering and helplessness? Yet, there have been religious martyrs who have thanked G-d for their hardship, because it gave them the ability to prove their faith. There are people lying in hospital beds who have inspired their families and followers with their faith, optimism and love, who have allowed their loved ones to elevate themselves by sharing these "worst of times" with them.

Recently I visited an old woman as she lay dying in a hospital. She had spent many Sabbath afternoons as a guest in my house, and I'd been neglectful in not visiting her earlier.

"Boy," she joked when she saw me, "the doctors must think the angel of death is coming soon if you're here to visit." I was a little thrown by her words, so I just sat there making small talk, gazing at the many tubes now running in and out of her once mobile body. I finally left with an immense feeling of hollowness. Then, in the elevator, a thought occurred to me, and I went back to see her again.

"Brenda," I said, "you know how proud you were that you kept faith even when you lost your first husband in the war and then again when your beloved second husband died? You know how you inspired so many people with your stories? Well, Brenda, now you can really win the World Series. As you know better than anyone else, life is nothing but a series of challenges. The little we accomplish while we're active is nothing compared to G-d's whole universe. But, here in this hospital bed, by keeping faith, you're accomplishing more, and challenging G-d to reciprocate, because your challenge is bigger. So, in a way, you're more alive now than ever. Don't give it up, Brenda, until it's over!"

"You think I don't know that, Mr. Big Shot?" she joked. "I'm not giving up anything! Still, it's nice to see you've learned a little something from the old lady."

My friend died a couple of weeks later, but I went to her funeral a lot more satisfied for our few extra words.

Failure, you see, *doesn't matter*. It's the *response* to failure that's important. In my business, I try to hire only two kinds of people: those who, like Joseph, are obsessed in some area of their lives, who perform a certain task with such vigor that I can literally feel the intensity and imagine what that life force could mean for us if properly channeled; the other group consists of individuals who have just had profound failures, screw-ups on an astonishingly grand level. That group includes people whose businesses collapsed because they gambled and lost, whose new technologies failed to gain market acceptance, whose companies have literally crashed and burned under their guidance. "So what," I tell myself, "it could have happened to anyone." Look how far they came before the crash! Look what talent and daring they possessed!

Everyone who's built a successful organization knows there's always a time when, in order to get ahead, you've got to overextend yourself. When you're literally out there alone on a tightrope and a strong breeze one way or the other can blow you off. That I'm here and they're there may just be because I had slightly better balance or better luck. But think of the effort, the talent it took to get there. Wow, if you could harness that kind of magic and bring it in-house, then watch out!

There is a problem though. Often, having lost everything, having fallen so low after rising so high, these individuals come to me broke and depressed. At this stage of their lives, they don't seem ready to confront any giants or scale any lofty heights. But looks can be deceptive. A person may be down but not out. What once burned brightly is almost always re-ignitable. I always hire these guys, both for their promise and, frankly, also because of my feeling for the brotherhood of humanity. You know, there but for the grace of G-d go I.

With a little nurturing, with a little time, being part of a winning team, these guys always start to thrive. Soon they're back to their old selves. It's never failed. I may have taken them on in part out of a charitable motive, but I've always wound up the real beneficiary, carried along on their shoulders and by their dreams.

This is true more than I'd like to admit, actually—because life does come full circle. Hiring people who have hit bottom has often worked out well for my business, but I can also personally empathize. You see, there was a time in my life when I also fell and broke and had to be carried. The only thing was, when I fell, I fell lower than anyone I ever met.

✦　　✦　　✦

My depression started in late 1992. I'm not sure what triggered it, although I can guess. I was under tremendous strain at work, trying to launch one business and keep another one going. The older business was an old-fashioned, reasonably profitable, small, conservative type of concern, just a dozen or so employees, the kind of place where everyone's like family. You hire maybe one new guy a year and everybody pitches in to do the same things year after year.

We operated out of a small building in the Bronx that I shared with my father's insurance agency. Every day at 11 a.m. a different one of us would go upstairs to prepare a healthy lunch in the upstairs kitchen. Then we'd all sit down together to eat (and study Talmud) for an hour or more. Afternoons, my dad would come sit by my desk, and we'd "talk business" and shoot the breeze for another hour or so. This had been my routine for over a decade. It was safe and comfortable. I wasn't suffering financially. I was living in a sort of womb.

Then I went into the telecommunications business. It started small, but soon I was hiring one or two new high-powered employees a week. Newspapers and magazines started writing articles about us. Big investors joined us. I soon had a large staff, with a lot of equipment and a big budget to meet. We didn't all fit together in our little Bronx building, not physically and not emotionally. The go-go telecom guys and the more laid-back staff from the original business had little in common.

The telecom guys ate lunch at their desk and grimaced when I went upstairs to have lunch and study with my old friends. My dad just shook his head when we spoke about my new business, baffled at how I could be involved in taking people's money and putting it into a project that lost cash each week. And the bigger the telecom business grew, the less we fit, and the more polarized my life became.

Finally I announced that I was moving the telecom operation fifteen miles away to a larger facility in New Jersey. Not wanting to separate from my father or uproot my older "family" business, I kept the old operation in the Bronx. That's when I really started to feel torn apart.

Every day I'd spend the morning at one business and the afternoon at the other. Wherever I was, they seemed to need me in the other place. I was always traveling back and forth in the car, available to no one. I finally forbade anyone from one office to call me at the other. I was trying to live in two different worlds. Then I stopped commuting back and forth and spent three days a week at the old place and two days at the new.

Soon, when the growth and demands of the telecom business changed this balance to three days there and two days at the old place, the old guys started sulking, and felt that I had abandoned them. And the look on my dad's face let me know he was accepting my gradual abandonment, as well. I felt emotionally torn. I tried to reassure everyone, tried to let everyone know that I was still the plain old Howard, that all the media attention and high finance didn't matter, that my identity was unchanged. I tried to reassure them and I tried to reassure myself, but it wasn't working. My identity was being torn away. The demands on me were growing. I started bringing the tension home with me. I couldn't relax. The double life was getting to be too much.

Finally I decided to bite the bullet and move the original business to New Jersey too. The old guys weren't happy, so I had to put the "myth" of family to sleep and tell them that was my decision and it was final. No more upstairs kitchen and family lunch. My dad must have been devastated. He didn't complain, but inside I felt I was killing him.

"Don't worry," I told him, "I'll visit every week for lunch."

"Sure," I imagined he must have been crying internally. "Sure you will. Goodbye, my little boy."

I was racked with guilt and I felt overwhelmed by work. Not only that, but the new business was burning money like crazy, and it seemed I was going broke and constantly begging for cash. For this I had given up my identity?

Then one night, not long after the move to the new office had been completed, my father told me he'd been diagnosed with cancer.

Oh my G-d, no! And my first thought: Did I

cause this? Even if I didn't, what did it matter? I had given up my time with my father, my best friend, and now I'd have no father.

I went into a tailspin. The pressure was too much. I cracked.

Even though my father's original diagnosis proved, thank G-d, to be wrong, for me it was too late. I just shut down physically and emotionally. I couldn't function. I couldn't eat. I began to cry uncontrollably. I couldn't sleep— that was the worst. After days of not sleeping, I couldn't function at all. Everything scared me. I was afraid of answering the phone. I was afraid of people seeing me this way.

I went to see a psychiatrist. All I could do was cry and wail for the loss of what I used to be. I told him I might be suicidal. He put me on drugs—they turned out to be the wrong drugs, the worst drugs for my condition. I lived only for my next session. I needed to go every day but could only schedule three times a week. This was the center of my life. I'd go to work, lock myself in a private room, think about what used to be and count the minutes until I could go downtown to see my psychiatrist and cry. Being able to do nothing else, I'd always arrive early at the psychiatrist's office and sit in my car, shaking and crying and waiting.

Forget about running a business. Forget about being a husband or father. Somehow everyone—my wife, my kids, my co-workers—all covered for me as I just kept spiraling downward. All I could think of was just parking the car and jumping off the George Washington Bridge. My wife said she'd never forgive me, and the kids would blame themselves and be scarred forever. What did we do wrong? they'd think. Why was daddy willing to leave us and kill himself? Great, I thought. I'm stuck living. Still I kept thinking of the bridge.

Finally, I changed doctors, and he changed my medications. "You're not a loser," he kept telling me. "Do something. Exercise. Get back your confidence. Just see me twice a week."

Slowly things started to get a little better. Just a little. Where I had gone from running every day to not being able to walk outside at all, I now forced myself to trudge through the snow. I forced myself to eat. I forced myself to see one or two people a day. I forced myself to pose for a magazine picture. But then I'd collapse, trembling, and throw up and start to slide. So I'd go back and see my shrink and try to get it together. This happened again and again. Each time I'd fall, I'd feel a little more worthless and a little more convinced my misery would never end.

It was summer and I was still struggling. I went to Israel on vacation, and was kept just barely functional by the prospect of my twice-weekly scheduled phone calls with my shrink.

Then one day a remarkable, seemingly trivial thing happened. I sent my kids to camp, as usual, and took my wife to some Bedouin mineral baths by the Dead Sea. I believe there are happy and unhappy places in the world, those that exude good energy and those that exude bad energy. For me, the Dead Sea was always one of the best places. I hoped the sea and the baths would help me.

But when things go bad, they usually just get worse and worse. Fear and feelings of worthlessness gripped me. The hell that held me in its clutches my mind just wouldn't leave me.

There, at the baths, my car died. Can you believe it? There I was, in the baking desert sun, with no one around but some Bedouins with camels, and my car died.

Then the Bedouins left.

"Great," my wife said, disgusted with me and the whole situation. "It's hopeless. What are we going to do now?"

Hopeless. Yes, it was hopeless. A useless car, a useless husband, and nowhere to turn for help. Then, suddenly, a thought struck me. Hadn't I been in this situation before? Through the shadows and years, a scene came back to me: my father starting his old manual transmission car, being pushed by another car, dropping the gears into second and suddenly the engine turning over. Then I began to picture it: rolling down a big hill into second and suddenly the motor turning over.

Yes. Yes. I could visualize it! If only I could find a hill to roll down, here at the bottom of this valley, here at the lowest point on the earth. And then I saw it. It was not a hill, but more like a ridge—just knee high, just before the sea. If I could just push the car to that ridge. It was probably impossible, but what else was there to do?

I don't know how it happened. I don't know where I, who could barely eat, sleep or walk, found the strength to push the car up the ridge. I don't know what instantly prompted me to stick my foot out the door and give one last extra push which accelerated the vehicle just a little bit more, just a little extra as we went over that ridge. I don't know if G-d was looking down and saying, "OK, this is it, the last stop, time to save him." I don't know anything. All I know is suddenly the motor coughed, turned over, and the car started. I hit the clutch, turned away from the sea and gunned the engine.

Then I did something I hadn't done for half a year. I grabbed my wife's hand, and a feeling of self-confidence started to flood through me. I began to laugh. We both began to laugh. I had started the car! I wasn't worthless after all!

I was all alone in the baking sun at the lowest point on earth, at the lowest point in my life, and I had just pushed that car over the last ridge in existence and the darn thing had started. I had started the car! It was dead as a doornail and I had started it.

And you know what? That car was me. If that car could be started, then so could I.

As we drove up the mountains back to Jerusalem and the temperature moderated, I periodically squeezed my wife's hand and smiled and, through semi-teary eyes, just repeated, "We started the car."

As unbelievable as it may sound, my motor started too. Not all at once. It coughed. It jerked. It shook. And then it started to really run. I started to run again too, and also to do other forms of exercise. I started to eat, and to spend time with my kids.

At the office, I moved out of my small room and back onto the general sales floor. I began speaking before groups again. I cut the shrink down to once a week. I cut my consumption of pills in half. Then I told the shrink that, although I truly appreciated his saving my life, I wasn't going to come anymore. I'd will myself to stand on my own two feet. He told me, "Good luck. I don't think you're ready, but good luck. My door is always open."

Many times during the first few months after I left him, I was ready to go back, but I got over it. Soon there was no way to tell that I'd been in the junkyard for close to a year. It was almost like I'd been completely refurbished. I was as good as new.

Well, maybe not quite. You never fully get over some things. The experience always stays with you. In fact, it marks you.

My experience, though, says so much about the human ability to meet challenges and overcome adversity. It is this resilience that is the greatness of man. Sure, everybody takes notice and is impressed with successful men when they're on a roll, when they go from triumph to triumph, when their stock price soars and their wealth climbs into the stratosphere, when every newspaper or magazine you pick up is filled with stories of their latest exploits. Then everyone is patting you on the back and wants you at their parties or as their friend. I know. I've been there. I'm there now.

But really, going from victory to victory when the wind's at your back, your bank accounts full to overflowing, and everyone wants to deal with you, is no remarkable talent. It's just doing your job and acting out your role. It doesn't really demonstrate courage, strength or character. It's nothing to be really proud of.

You know what I'm proud of? Forcing myself to walk through the snow and forcing myself to go to work and deal with people, when every interaction with people scared me. I was terrified just to hear the phone ring. I'm proud of driving over the George Washington Bridge again and again when I felt all alone and only desired to drive off it. *That* truly took strength and character—being all alone and facing my own personal monster.

Believe me, when you face a challenge like that, you *are* all alone, just you and G-d. And you talk to yourself plenty and pray plenty. You ask yourself endless questions, like: What really matters? What are you most afraid of and why? Who's a real friend and who's a phony? Which values matter? What do you want to accomplish in life? What are your real capabilities? How best to use them? How can you make the world better? And how can you come to enjoy life again?

These are excellent questions. It's good to confront them and come face to face with yourself. It's crucial to truly know yourself and reform the parts you don't like. In this world, where each of us is barraged with an unrelenting stream of facts and images (and sometimes garbage) concerning other people and their expectations, it's good to have that self-knowledge, and to find truth and G-dliness within yourself. Maybe this is one of the best reasons to confront a challenge—to allow oneself to face the truth and to learn that you can live with that truth.

Ever notice how often great baseball players talk to themselves before they step up to bat? Well, successful businesspeople, artists, and statesmen all do the same, in one form or another, before they face their own challenges.

But when the challenge is severe and threatens to overwhelm you, as it did me, when it becomes so monstrous that you think you won't be able to handle it without some kind of miracle, then even many avowedly non-religious people do one more thing. They pray. They turn to G-d and, with all their might, they ask for some kind of intervention to help them. And it's one of my firmest beliefs that G-d hears each and every sincere prayer and responds, though rarely by actually changing reality and turning the tide. More often, He answers these prayers by giving a person the *strength* to deal with his or her difficulties and often to come back even stronger and better than before.

I believe this is what happened to me. I came back. I'm a survivor. Since then, my wife and I have had four more beautiful children who have filled our lives with joy. Since then we've also made new, wonderful friends. I've danced at weddings and laughed at shows. My companies have gone public. Our stock price has soared. I've written a book that has sold widely. I've been privileged to give much money to charity and have started several new charitable organizations on my own. Colleges, universities and other worthwhile organizations have invited me to sit on their boards.

All my prayers were answered, though I was not necessarily granted the things for which I prayed. Nevertheless, everything turned out for the best, just like I believe everything in the world ultimately turns out for the best.

The Roman Empire collapsed. Genghis Khan was wiped out. Hitler lost. Stalin's empire is no more. From the ashes of the Holocaust, Israel was born. Now, after the overthrow of communism, liberty and democracy are beginning to make inroads in some of the most oppressed parts of the world.

And yet I, and perhaps all thinking people, still feel more like a survivor than a victor. If you asked me whether getting where I am today is worth the price I had to pay, I don't know what I'd answer. And that's only because I wouldn't give up for anything the children we had after my depression (or any of my children, for that matter).

If you eliminated that, though, and just asked me about the wealth, the power, the fame, was it worth it, I'd tell you in a minute, hell no, no way. I'd never relive that nightmare for anything. I'd never exchange the unquestioning happiness, optimism and illusions of omnipotence that I've lost forever for the reality of success. If I could go back to 1992 and just lead a plain, happy life, I'd do it in a minute.

But this wasn't my choice. I'm also sure that no survivor of the Holocaust, no matter how successful, or however happy he or she must be about Israel's existence, would choose any differently. Do me a favor, they would tell G-d, take back your present and take back the horror and death and misery too. But clearly it's not their choice either.

The only choice any of us have is what to do with the present: to be good, to be indifferent, or to be evil; to rise to challenges or to flee from them; to share in the work of perfecting the world or just throw up our hands in surrender. Frankly, I thank G-d we're free to choose. And I also think the choice is clear.

twelve

How I *got* *where* I *am*

NO ONE GROWS UP IN A VACUUM. WE ALL HAVE ROLE models who have shaped our lives and values.

When I was a little boy, my grandmother was my best friend. That didn't change as I got older, though by the time she died I was married, and Debbie—the girl she'd welcomed into her home over a decade earlier—had not only become my wife, but my closest friend, as well. My marriage to Debbie, though, in no way diminished my grandmother's special status. When the time came to order her tombstone, I insisted that our friendship be added to the inscription.

I visit her grave occasionally. It's on the side of a hill in Mount Hebron Cemetery. I go usually with my wife, often with a couple of my children. And the part on the stone about our friendship—it breaks me up a little inside every time I read it.

My grandmother and I did everything together. When I learned to drive, I'd take her and my Great (really great) Aunt Anna, her sister and longtime roommate, for rides in the country. We'd go out to eat, or I'd bring Chinese food up to the house, or more often they'd insist on cooking for me. We'd discuss business or family politics, and I'd install an air conditioner for them or put some Depression-era plate back on a high shelf they couldn't reach.

On New Year's Eves, from the time Debbie and I started dating and even into the early years of our marriage, we would leave whatever party we were attending early so we could watch the ball drop with them. Afterwards, we'd have hors d'oeuvres and champagne, and Grandma and Aunt Anna—then in their eighties—would stand up with their knee warmers in place, kick up their legs as much as their arthritis would allow, and dance the Can Can for us. Since they've died, I try to avoid doing anything special on New Year's Eve. It's just not the same.

It was long before I got my driver's license, though, that my grandmother and I really bonded. One of the most memorable experiences of my life was when I was a little boy and would spend almost every weekend on an overnight at Grandma's. We'd open the sofa bed as soon as I arrived on Friday night and then two days of non-stop partying would begin.

We'd watch TV late into the night— wrestling shows when my Grandpa was still alive, Rudy Vallee movies afterward. We'd play Power and Grandma would cheat. We'd make egg omelets with a special hand eggbeater. We'd pack picnics and go to the park. Then we'd shop in a store that still killed the chickens on the spot, and we'd buy from fruit vendors who put special produce aside for favored customers. We'd come home, have ice cream sundaes, which Aunt Anna covered in Rice Krispies and pineapple jelly "because it's healthy that way," or we'd have Jello containing grated coconut and pineapple chunks, for the same reason. Then we'd wash clothes on the washboard and make supper. By then, I was so tired I couldn't even stay awake for TV.

But the next morning, bright and early, it

was time to get the Sunday paper with the color comics, read the funny pages, then go for a brisk morning walk with Aunt Anna—"because it's healthy."

Later, Dad, Mom and my sister would come to take us all for a drive in the country. After our drive, I'd help Grandma and Aunt Anna cook up a really special meal of potato latkes and fried chicken for the whole family. After dinner we'd all watch "The Jackie Gleason Show" on TV, have coffee, cake and baked apples that Aunt Anna made with walnuts and dates, "because it's healthier that way," and we'd all go home.

I not only had a terrific time, I learned a lot, and not just about greasy cooking with "healthy" side dishes. I learned about character, strength and self-sacrifice. I witnessed how someone could go from being a wealthy man's wife to a widow with a young child in the Depression. How one goes from living carefree in a big house to taking in borders to stave off foreclosure. I learned how a person could work day and night in an unheated newsstand to feed her son and also raise her kid brother. How one can remarry to give her son a father while silently suffering because the flame had never died for her first love. I learned how someone could endure all this hardship and never complain, and just brim with joy at the sight of grandchildren.

There were other things I learned, too: what it was like to be born in and grow up on New York's Lower East Side, a poor area, teeming with immigrants; how much the American dream can mean to someone from this background and how much pride one can have in her kid brother's heroics in World War II; and how wrong it is for the people whom you helped when you were on top to forget about you when you're down.

I also learned the reality of being poor. What it's like never to buy anything unless it's on sale or with a coupon, to make your own clothes, to turn out the lights whenever you leave a room.

But I learned that there could be joy in such a life too. The joy of shopping for bargains, cooking from scratch, doing the cleaning on the washboard and watching it dry over the tub. It's a rich and pungent sort of life, more loving and communal in a way than the more processed, prepared, ready-to-consume life of the more well-to-do.

Though I was a baby boomer, it was through my grandmother that I received the values and life lessons of someone who went through the Depression. Still, my dreams and aspirations were those of my generation. For one, there were no Lower East Side limitations on my aspirations. I was a baby boomer, part of the generation that was going to the moon. I'd be rich, famous, powerful. I told my parents I was planning to be President of the United States, a famous inventor and the world's richest businessman, all at the same time.

"All at the same time," my father ribbed, "or one at a time?"

I chafed at his comment. All at the same time, and why not? I shared a lot with my grandmother but clearly not her sense of limitation or her finite dreams.

This came home to me one Sunday morning when I was thirteen. I'd just spent the previous two nights at her apartment. Today, however, unlike our usual schedule, I wouldn't be spending Sunday with her. I'd just gotten my first job as a helper and delivery boy at an Italian butcher shop in my neighborhood, and Sunday was my first day.

I was feeling pretty grown up and excited. My own job. My own salary. Who knew what this could lead to? Mansions on the water and ticker tape parades seemed almost within grasp. At last I was leaving childhood behind and starting on my own road. How I had waited for this day!

And yet, as my grandmother walked me from her housing project, through her run-down neighborhood filled with boarded up stores, to the stop from which I'd catch a bus to my own much more affluent neighborhood, where my job awaited me, a certain sadness and nostalgia swept over me. I was going off on my own to travel the road I'd always wanted to travel. But I was leaving my grandmother behind, physically and metaphorically. The butcher shop I would be working at was open on Saturday as well as Sunday. So, except for the occasional day off, there wouldn't be the fun weekends together anymore. The picnics in the park, the Rice Krispies sundaes. But I wasn't sad for myself. I was sad for her.

I was the joy of her life. Her hopes and dreams were embodied in me. And yet, as I left to fulfill those dreams, I'd be leaving her behind, going on a journey she never took and never could take. She was an old woman on a limited income whose whole life was circumscribed by these few blocks of boarded-up stores. I was a young boy off on this bright sunshiny morning on a bus ride through tree-lined streets that could take me anywhere.

Suddenly, it didn't seem like such a spectacular day after all. It felt more like a funeral. Just my old grandmother, uncomplaining as usual, walking me to the bus stop that would take me away forever. As I boarded the bus and it started to pull away, I looked out of the back window of the bus at my grandma, arthritic and hunched over, pulling her old shopping cart to look for bargains on the avenue. Old, arthritic, a little unsteady and, now, alone.

I just put down my head and started to cry.

I teared all through the ghetto until it was time to change buses. Then we pulled onto the parkway. As the sun shone through the trees, I started to get excited about my new job at the butcher shop, excited about all the things that would happen and all the things I'd do. The things hadn't even happened yet, and already I was excited to call my grandmother that night and tell her about them. I was sure she couldn't wait to hear about it. That was how much I knew she loved me.

✦   ✦   ✦

Although my father's mother was my best friend, I had another grandmother who also had an equally powerful effect on me. We called her Bubby, Yiddish for grandma. She was my mother's mother and her principal language was Yiddish, the language that Jews spoke in Eastern Europe. Although Bubby lived in America, had raised her children here and would have carried an American passport had she ever traveled overseas, Bubby was clearly still a part of

Eastern Europe, a part that just somehow ended up in the Bronx. Actually, if Bubby hadn't unwillingly landed in the Bronx, she'd have been murdered by the Nazis just as her parents and nine of her eleven siblings were.

Bubby's fate was different. A year before the war, a middle-aged Polish immigrant, who'd made it in the States, returned to Poland to find a bride from the Old Country—a religious Jewish girl from a traditional family untainted by the modern ways of the *goldene*, but *treife medina* (the golden but unkosher land).

My Bubby, twenty years younger than my grandfather, was just the type of young girl he had in mind. But Bubby didn't want to go. She didn't want to leave her mama, her home and her traditions to travel with this wealthy older stranger to a strange new land. But her Papa said go and, in Poland, Papa's word was law. So the Rabbi was called, some chickens were killed and wine obtained for the wedding feast, and a week later the reluctant young bride packed up her Sabbath candles and a few other possessions, bid her family a tearful goodbye and left with her rich American husband to America.

Well, maybe not so rich. In fact, not rich at all. He lived, in fact, in the Bronx, and he was just a poor storekeeper selling lox, herring and pickles. All that had happened was that Bubby moved from the shtetl in Eastern Europe to a different one in the Bronx.

She kept strictly to her "Old World" religion her whole life, lighting her Sabbath candles, and giving her husband three children.

Nothing really changed much when my grandfather died, leaving her with children who were still young and at home. Now, instead of working at the store to barely get by, she barely got by working as a cleaning lady in the Empire State building. Not on the Sabbath though; the Sabbath was holy. Then she'd stay home, eat the strictly kosher food she ate all week (but never heated on the Sabbath) and pray to G-d for the souls of her family, almost all of whom had been killed in the Holocaust.

The terrible events going on in the world had no impact on Bubby's faith. They may have torn her up physically and emotionally, but her faith was untouched. This was true even later when all her children ignored the Sabbath and abandoned the dietary laws. They were Americans, part of the New World, she must've thought. She loved them just the same. For her, though, G-d was G-d, the law was the law, and the ways of the Old World were still binding.

I never remember Bubby being a vibrant, healthy woman, going for brisk walks like Grandma. But after Bubby's colostomy operation, which she had when I was five, she was terribly limited. She even had to live in our living room for months while she recuperated. It was during this time, however, that we really bonded. Bubby didn't want the operation. She would have preferred to die than to live with a bag. But my dad sort of pushed her into it. I'm glad because I would never have picked up her values if my father would've let her slip away then. He was able to push her into the operation with the same basic argument my wife used against me when I was thinking about jumping off the George Washington Bridge: "You've got to live for the children."

So they put a TV into the living room while Bubby recuperated and every Tuesday night we'd howl together at the antics of Red Skelton. In fact, every night we'd watch Bubby's favorite programs together. Every night but Friday night. On the Sabbath, Bubby lit her candles, mumbled her prayers, ate a little food she'd prepared earlier in her own pot (she couldn't use ours because they weren't kosher) and went to sleep without watching TV.

Bubby prepared many dishes for me in her own pots and pans. Sweet and sour *flanken* and cabbage, matzah meal latkes and square yellow sugar cookies that never went stale. She would prepare dishes for us, but she'd never eat anything made in our non-kosher kitchen. Even at the Passover Seder, which I was so anxious for her to attend, Bubby just had a matzah and a banana.

I wanted her to attend the Seder because I wanted her to see that I was religious too, that I also had respect for ritual and tradition, and that the faith that she held fast to against the seemingly unstoppable tide of modernity was one I also respected. In short, I wanted Bubby to know that her values had been passed on to me.

I wanted her to understand that more than just intellectual values, she'd passed on her faith and her commitment to observance of all the Jewish traditions. I began to believe that her direct connection to G-d gave her almost mystical powers to affect people's lives. No wonder—look how profoundly this old woman, who could barely walk from room to room, affected my life.

thirteen

The chain

WHAT I ULTIMATELY GLEANED FROM BOTH MY Grandma and my Bubby is that they and I are part of a chain. Their lives and potentials were limited: by time, by place, and by background. They were old; they'd come from poverty and were uneducated. The middle-class America in which I was raised was a strange place to them. And yet they were full of values and experiences I would never have, the product of thousands of years of struggle and ethical refinement. Without them, I would be a creature of the moment, an achievement machine whose only true values would be expediency and pragmatism, whose only purpose would be to satisfy my immediate needs.

And someday, I'd be old too, an anachronism living in a world different from the one in which I grew up, a world full of young people running everything with values far different from my own.

What really, I wondered, is the purpose of life other than to pass on your values? Without this, I realized, one's life would be meaningless, just a vanishing set of experiences, acquisitions and feelings. Simply having children and grand-children, just making new human protoplasm without passing on your values to them, would also be meaningless. What would be the meaning of having people around after you're gone, who look vaguely like you but with whom you'd have no values in common?

Are the businessmen descendants of Karl Marx or the left-leaning progeny of Rockefeller any kind of legacy for their ancestors? From Marx's and Rockefeller's points of view, these descendants could just as well have been hatched from eggs.

In past times of historical continuity, when little changed from one century to the next, these issues may *not* have been of such conse-quence. Serfs gave birth to serfs, noblemen always had noblemen for children and every generation more or less repeated the life cycles of their antecedents. Each generation naturally

looked to the past for guidance, since the problems they had to deal with were little different
from past problems.

But as the pace of change has accelerated,
the tendency has been to ignore the past and
think that new values need to be formulated for
new circumstances or that perhaps in such
shifting sands morality needs to be totally
revamped.

The generation in which we now live has
seen change on an unrivaled scale, perhaps
more change in my brief lifetime than in all of
previously recorded time. Where once in a few
centuries an ancestor might change his family's
destiny by leaving his native land, today we jet
back and forth across oceans and continents at
a moment's notice. Where people once went to
see a play once a year or once in a lifetime, now
new TV programs are aired every thirty minutes
on fifty or more stations. CNN and the *New York
Times* deliver more news in a day than people in
the past had to assimilate in a lifetime.

In my grandmother's life, she saw the inven-
tion and proliferation of the airplane, the

automobile, radio, television, computers, to say nothing of the washing machines and dryers she never used. As a young girl she saw most deliveries made with a horse, but together we watched men walk on the moon. She saw the rise and fall of the Kaiser, Hitler and Stalin. She heard Churchill inspire England to fight for their finest hour and Franklin Delano Roosevelt encourage America by telling them they had nothing to fear but fear itself. She witnessed people selling apples on street corners during the Depression and saw stocks like IBM rocket in the '60s. She saw Kennedy shot.

How could anyone live through that much? But you know what? In my lifetime the speed of change has only increased. So how can anyone hold onto reality from one moment to the next? Many people just try to ride life like they ride a surfboard on a tidal wave. Forget about the last wave, the last instant; just try to stay upright for the moment. Think about an instant ago and you'll be capsized by the wave you're now riding. People are so focused on the present and unmindful of the past that most watches no longer have hands. The movement of the hands of a watch tells you the present is just a step along the way from the past. Today, most watches are digital. It's 12:58, they say, and thus convey a hidden message: Live for the present.

And yet, isn't this just insane? Just because everything's moving faster, have fundamental truths really changed? Don't we all need to absorb G-d's eternal values—the values of the Bible—in order to deal righteously with the present, fast-moving as it may be? Isn't it the special obligation of a generation that has lived through so much change to work even harder to pass on the experiences of our elders?

When I was a little boy I met many people with numbers on their arms, numbers that had been tattooed in Auschwitz and Buchenwald. Can anyone fathom what these people lived through? Can anyone deny that they have an enormous amount to teach us about man's capacity for hatred, for survival, faith and rebirth?

I was privileged to have been born into the generation that could still learn firsthand from these people. Back when I was in my early twenties, I chose a seat in the synagogue in the area where these survivors would sit and talk with each other. They recounted barefoot escapes through frozen forests with Gestapo bullets and dogs literally at their heels. They'd recount hunger and courage in the concentration camps and the families that weren't there when they arrived home. They'd tell of their struggle to reclaim their lives, and through their embrace of life they conveyed to me more about the value of life than any philosopher could communicate.

They sat near the front of the synagogue, uncomfortably close to where the Rabbi speaks from but, in their midst, I never felt discomfort. Recently, though, after twenty years, I've changed my seat to a more innocuous location in the back. Fellow congregants sometimes ask why I've moved. "Well, I can talk back here with my friend during the sermon without getting into trouble," I quip.

Actually, I'm lying to them. The truth is, over the last twenty years almost all my survivor friends have passed away. All the experiences, the talk, the special zest for life they shared are gone. Now, with just their memories there, I'm uncomfortable and I feel like I need to talk.

I have a special obligation, you see, to keep their memories and their life lessons alive. I need to share their experiences and wisdom with my contemporaries, with the next generation and the one after that. That's what continuity is about.

I have an obligation to share the values and memories of my Grandmother, my Bubby, and the World War II vets I know. I have an obligation to share my memories of the day Kennedy was shot and how America turned on itself in Vietnam and with Watergate. I have an obligation to tell what the Six Day War and Israel's recapture of Jerusalem meant to Jews alive at that time, and what it meant to us all when a man walked on the moon and when the Berlin Wall came down.

But these memories are just fragmented pieces of a whole tapestry. To relate them, even to pass them on without also giving a context—a belief system into which they fit—would be meaningless. Without context, future generations could easily either forget these isolated memories or use them to support an approach that is inconsistent with the true meaning of the events.

The bodies are barely cold from the Holocaust and already some revisionist historians are using photos of the camps to attempt to show that the Nazis were the real victims. The tank tracks are barely gone from Tiananmen Square and already an American president, more concerned with economic gain than ultimate truth is congratulating the Chinese on their moves toward democracy.

Enough already! Doesn't truth matter?

A good question. Truth *does* matter. But to see it, mankind must have a belief system rooted in truth, a belief system that doesn't change from day to day.

The Bible, to my mind, is the best such belief system there is. It has stood the test of time, and any system that dares to call itself moral—like the liberty-loving doctrines of the American founding fathers—has its roots in the Bible.

Against the values set down by G-d in the

Bible, "truths of the moment" can be judged, and events can be put into their correct context. The Bible can create a context for meaningfully passing down memories to the next generation.

This is an important point. If humanity is one long historical chain, and if, therefore, one of the major purposes in life is to pass your experience and knowledge to the next generation, then raising your children to adhere to your religion and values is essential. Were you to come back hundreds of years from now and sit with your great-great-great-grandchildren, you'd have satisfaction not only from the fact that they somewhat resembled you, but also that they shared your values and were still working toward their fulfillment. What greater satisfaction could you possibly hope for?

epilogue

AND SO, MY FRIENDS, WE'VE COME FULL CIRCLE. In these few pages, we've dealt with nearly all the deep questions of the ages.

We've looked at such questions as: Is there a G-d? And if there is, why does He let evil exist and allow the righteous to suffer? We've reviewed what we should do with our lives and what our ultimate purpose is. Hopefully my explanations have satisfied you.

Just to recap: There is a G-d. He is the source of all morality, and our freedom is all-important to Him. Evil exists and sometimes the righteous suffer because otherwise free will would have no meaning. Our job in life is to continuously undertake challenges and confront evil, so that we will grow as people, and so that we can help move the world closer to the goodness, and further from the evil, that G-d gave us the freedom to create.

All along we must pass on to the next

generation values and experience that we've gained from our own challenges and from the challenges of those who came before us.

Oh yeah, just one more thing. Besides all the serious stuff—enjoy life. With all the suffering, all the injustice and all the evil, it's important to keep in mind that there's a lot more good in the world. For every starving person, there are thousands more who are eating what they like best. For each unemployed person, there are dozens getting satisfaction from productive work. For every heartbroken person, there are many more in love.

And you know what? With effort on their part or perhaps on ours, tomorrow these same downtrodden individuals could be well fed, gainfully employed and, yes, even in love. Yesterday's hardship will be remembered as just a bump along the road, a little hill that makes reaching the summit all the more satisfying.

Remember that G-d wants us to be happy and enjoy life. He's the one who made food tasty, love sweet and work satisfying. He created all the pleasures of the world for us to enjoy.

G-d knows what He's doing. He set up the world in such a way that these pleasures would motivate us to ultimately choose good.

Don't forget: Food is tastier when it's earned by one's honest effort.

Love, which involves giving, is much deeper and more satisfying than a relationship in which one just receives.

Freedom is more precious when people have to work and sacrifice for it. In fact, in almost all things, the righteous path, the path of challenge, leads to greater satisfaction, deeper understanding and relationships, and more enduring results.

So go for it. Enjoy yourself, and not just a little. Deeply. Suck in all the satisfaction life has in store for you. And when there's no more left, take comfort in knowing that not only did you experience life's greatest satisfactions while you were here, but, more importantly, you gave to the world as well, and hopefully your contributions will let future generations have even deeper satisfaction and enjoyment from this world.

And one last thing. Be careful. Don't be a

dummy. Wear your seat belt. Cross on the green. And don't ever drink and drive. G-d doesn't want us to be road kill. He wants us here to take and to give all that life has to offer. He doesn't want us going out in the rain without an umbrella and getting pneumonia. He wants us to listen to the weather forecast. That's probably why He invented meteorology and radio waves in the first place, so we'd know when a storm was coming and so the nitwits at Con Ed could make sure their lightning rods were really working.

Once people acknowledge how present G-d is in the world, they won't just attribute a really big miracle to the weather. When all the lights go out, people won't say it was just lightning. They'll realize the magnitude of what they're experiencing. With humanity torn away from the dependence on and worship of technology, people might join together by candlelight into one giant brotherhood, like they did in the great blackouts of 1965 and 2003. On the other hand, they could run amuck rioting and looting, like in the blackout of 1977. That's what free will is all about. So unless you really know what you're doing, leave the miracles to G-d and never, I mean never, stick your finger in an electric fan.